CADDIES & BOXES

COMPILED BY TONY CURTIS

First Published March 1977
Reprinted   Oct   1977
Revised Edition June   1978

Exchange rate $2 = £1 or rate
of exchange at time of auction.

Original Edition   ISBN 902921-42-8
Revised Edition   ISBN 902921-76-2

Published by Lyle Publications, Glenmayne, Galashiels, Scotland.
Distributed in the U.S.A. by Apollo, 391 South Road, Poughkeepsie, N.Y. 12601

INTRODUCTION

Congratulations! You now have in your hands an extremely valuable book. It is one of a series specially devised to aid the busy professional dealer in his everyday trading. It will also prove to be of great value to all collectors and those with goods to sell, for it is crammed with illustrations, brief descriptions and valuations of hundreds of antiques.

Every effort has been made to ensure that each specialised volume contains the widest possible variety of goods in its particular category though the greatest emphasis is placed on the middle bracket of trade goods rather than on those once - in - a - lifetime museum pieces whose values are of academic rather than practical interest to the vast majority of dealers and collectors.

This policy has been followed as a direct consequence of requests from dealers who sensibly realise that, no matter how comprehensive their knowledge, there is always a need for reliable, up-to-date reference works for identification and valuation purposes.

When using your Antiques and their Values to assess the worth of goods, please bear in mind that it would be impossible to place upon any item a precise value which would hold good under all circumstances. No antique has an exactly calculable value; its price is always the result of a compromise reached between buyer and seller, and questions of condition, local demand and the business acumen of the parties involved in a sale are all factors which affect the assessment of an object's 'worth' in terms of hard cash.

In the final analysis, however, such factors cancel out when large numbers of sales are taken into account by an experienced valuer, and it is possible to arrive at a surprisingly accurate assessment of current values of antiques; an assessment which may be taken confidently to be a fair indication of the worth of an object and which provides a reliable basis for negotiation.

Throughout this book, objects are grouped under category headings and, to expedite reference, they progress in price order within their own categories. Where the description states 'one of a pair' the value given is that for the pair sold as such.

Printed by Apollo Press, Dominion Way, Worthing, Sussex, England.
Bound by Newdigate Press, Vincent Lane, Dorking, Surrey, England.

CONTENTS

Victorian oval snuff box with agate inset hinged cover, 2in. wide, Birmingham 1857. $84 £42

George III gold-mounted agate vinaigrette, 1¼in. diameter, circa 1789. $320 £160

Vinaigrette with inside grille and agate top and base, ¾in. deep.
                                   $340 £170

French agate trinket box with ormolu mounts, circa 1830, 3½in. wide. $360 £180

A good cornelian box with ormolu mounts, 4 x 2¼in.
                         $430 £215

Early 19th century gold-mounted agate vinaigrette, 1¼in. wide, circa 1820. $560 £280

An attractive late 18th century patchwork agate box with ball feet. $660 £330

Late 18th century polished and shell carved agate snuff box with gold mounts, 2½in. wide. $1,700 £850

Wooden mouse trap. $4 £2

Mid 19th century 'Crystal Palace' brass birdcage. $110 £55

Small dog kennel in mahogany 21 in. long, with a detachable chain and brass collar engraved 'Toby'. $310 £155

Oak mouse trap. $320 £160

A very rare mahogany cat or dog kennel with detachable gable roof, 15in. long, 11in. high, 10in. wide. $360 £180

Gourd cricket-cage from the Ch'ien Lung period with tortoiseshell lid set in rosewood rim. $660 £330

A fine and rare George III mahogany cockfighting carrying cage. $1,680 £840

19th century ormolu birdcage with ogee top, 24in. high. $2,800 £1,400

Mahogany apothecary box complete with bottles, circa 1820. $100 £50

Mahogany medicine case fitted with glass jars, mortar and pestle, etc., 8¼in. wide. $130 £65

Late 18th century mahogany apothecary's box complete with the original bottles. $170 £85

Ship's apothecary chest complete with 'Seaman's Medical Friend'. $240 £120

A Victorian mahogany portable medicine chest, the front pair of deep doors opening to reveal velvet lined bottle racks and small fitted drawers, 1ft. wide. $240 £120

Outstanding George III mahogany apothecary's cabinet on bracket feet, with old bottles, pestle and mortar, 15in. high, circa 1795. $770 £385

An oak and metal bound wine cask with tap, 1ft.8in. $30 £15

Stoneware spirit barrel with brass tap. $70 £35

A steel banded oak cider barrel with hand rivetted joints to bands, 11in. diam. at top, circa 1840. $90 £45

Steel banded wooden corn measure, stamped KP, circa 1790, 16½in. diam, 14in. high. $116 £58

An attractive well made bucket, with wrought swing handle and decorative rivetted strength bands, circa 1790, 17in. high. $120 £60

Old oak rum barrel with brass straps, 21in. high. $180 £90

BIBLE BOXES

Chased brass Bible box in book form, 7¾in. wide. $40 £20

17th century oak Bible box. $80 £40

Carved oak oblong Bible box, 2ft.2in. wide. $100 £50

16th century oak Bible box. $120 £60

An oak Bible box with lunette carving on the front, circa 1700. $130 £65

An oak Bible box, showing the Stuart Coat-of-Arms, retaining the original hand-blocked lining paper. $190 £95

A very small oak Bible box, its front carved with a stylised tulip motif, circa 1680. $300 £150

17th century oak Bible box on stand. $320 £160

17th century oak Bible box complete with stand. $340 £170

Dark oak Bible box, circa 1600 on a stand of a later date. $360 £180

An oak Bible box, its front and sides carved with two rows of flutings, with a reeded edge to the top, circa 1600. $400 £200

Early oak Bible box on shaped legs. $500 £250

13

BISCUIT CONTAINERS

Victorian biscuit tin. $10 £5

W & R Jacob biscuit tin in the form of a Jacobean log box. $20 £10

Oak biscuit barrel with EPNS fittings and a ceramic lining, circa 1910. $24 £12

Huntley and Palmer biscuit tin. $36 £18

Huntley & Palmer pedestal biscuit tin decorated with classical figures. $20 £10

Huntley and Palmer tin decorated with printed paper, circa 1900. $24 £12

Huntley & Palmer laundry basket biscuit tin, circa 1904. $30 £15

Biscuit tin in the form of a cannon. $44 £22

A Britannia metal oval
biscuit box. $44 £22

Huntley and Palmer 'Book'
biscuit tin, 1924. $48 £24

Jacob's gypsy caravan biscuit
tin, circa 1905. $56 £28

Jacob & Co., Coronation coach
biscuit box, 1937. $56 £28

Huntley and Palmer 'Book'
biscuit tin, 1920. $60 £30

Huntley and Palmer library
biscuit tin. $68 £34

Library biscuit tin·by Huntley
and Palmer, 1900. $72 £36

A plated shell design biscuit
box on pierced end supports.
$110 £55

BOOKENDS

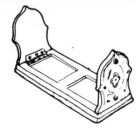

Victorian walnut and brass book slide. $24 £12

Early Victorian mahogany book-ends with ivory and brass decorations. $36 £18

A Tunbridge ware bookrack. $84 £42

Victorian rosewood bookends decorated with porcelain panels. $84 £42

19th century Tunbridge ware book rack. $96 £48

Victorian rosewood blotter and bookends with brass mounts and malachite patres. $144 £72

An elmroot inlaid box, the cover satinwood parquetry inlaid, 11¼in. $44 £22

A decorative wooden box in the form of a book, 7¾in. $30 £15

A Victorian rosewood box and cover with satinwood banded borders, 11in. wide. $44 £22

An Indian coromandel wood oblong box, the hinged cover ivory inlaid with a circular panel of flowers and an elephant, 14½in. $50 £25

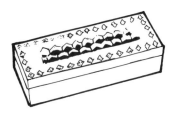

Victorian Tunbridge ware glove box with geometric design. $50 £25

A George III mahogany and brass oblong box, with brass handles and feet, 12in. wide. $70 £35

A mahogany box, with drawer and brass ring handles, on ball feet, 15in. wide. $72 £36

A fine brass banded mahogany box, with ivory label showing maker's name, Arnold and Sons, West Smithfield, London, circa 1830. $100 £50

Rectangular cloisonne box, circa 1925, blue background colour, 2½ x 5 x 3in. $116 £58

Napoleonic prisoner of war straw work box. $144 £72

An interesting African, probably Benin, carved oblong wood box, the lid carved with stylised European figure, 5 x 15 x 3in. $170 £85

Mahogany brass banded chest, the hinged lid inlaid with brass shield, by Edwards, James Street, London, circa 1800. $220 £110

A 17th century cedarwood box,
19 x 4½in. $530 £265

Mid 19th century French 'pietra
dura' ebony box, the raised top
and sides with a hardstone panel
of fruit and foliage within a
bronze border. $580 £290

A Micmac quilled birchbark box,
7½ x 6 x 5¼in. $600 £300

A small 17th century wrought
iron box. $1,800 £900

Dutch silver box, Leeuwarden
circa 1750, 22oz.10dwt.$3,600
£1,800

A very fine silver sweetmeat box,
maker's mark B.B., with a
crescent below, London 1676,
18.4cm., 21oz.12dwt. $40,000
£20,000

19

Victorian brass oblong snuff
box. $12 £6

Brass octagonal box with handle
on the cover, pierced. $24 £12

Japanese bronze oblong box with
bird head handles, 9½in. wide. $72 £36

A shaped brass casket with
ringed lion carrying handles
and standing on four claw and
ball feet, circa 1750, 8in. wide,
3½in. deep, 4½in. high. $120 £60

Late 17th century six sided brass
footwarmer, 13cm. high. $480 £240

Red bronze box with silver rims
and lining, the cover decorated
with the sixteen disciples of
Buddha. $2,400 £1,200

A Japanese lacquered miniature
cabinet, with three drawers,
cupboard and lidded compartments,
15in. high, 11½in. wide. $40 £20

19th century Chinese lacquered
and brass bound cabinet,
14 x 8in. $50 £25

A 19th century Chinese yellow
lacquer miniature cabinet,
enclosed by two doors, on stand.
                    $80 £40

A Japanese black lacquered
cabinet of five small drawers
enclosed by two doors,
decorated in gilt, 15in. high,
12in. wide. $80 £40

Small 19th century Japanese
lacquered cabinet of five
drawers, 30cm. wide. $110 £55

Miniature Japanese cabinet in
lacquer, with bird designs. $110 £55

A small 18th century Continental ebonised cabinet of drawers with mirror fronts, 23cm. wide. $116 £58

A miniature ivory parquetry inlaid and amboyna wood cabinet of drawers with brass carrying handles, 7½ x 6in. $120 £60

A Victorian rosewood and mother-of-pearl inlaid cabinet, the hinged top fitted as work box, one drawer fitted with writing slope, 14in. high, 12in. wide. $144 £72

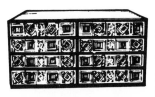

An Italian ebonised and walnut cabinet of eight small drawers, inlaid with ivory and with parquetry decoration, 2ft.7½in. wide, 15½in. high. $420 £210

Antique Spanish walnut-framed table top cabinet veneered with tortoiseshell panels with ivory borders, 16¼in. wide. $530 £265

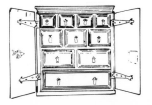

An old oak cabinet of ten small drawers formerly belonging to Queen Mary, from Holyrood Palace. $530 £265

A Ch'ien Lung black and gilt
lacquered dwarf cabinet, 3ft.8in.
wide. $820 £410

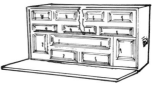

17th century Spanish walnut
vargueno with two iron locks
and handles, 45in. wide.$1,560 £780

German cabinet profusely inlaid
with two scenes, musical trophies
and flowers, 20½in. wide, circa
1600. $1,970 £985

Ebony and tortoiseshell-veneered
18th century Dutch cabinet,
depicting bible scenes. $7,260 £3,630

Early 20th century Italian
table cabinet by Carlo Bugatti.
                   $9,000 £4,500

17th century amber cabinet
from North Germany, 42in.
high. $38,500 £19,250

23

CARD CASES

Plain Victorian
silver card case.
$24 £12

Engraved silver card
case, hallmarked
Birmingham 1901.
$24 £12

Gentleman's silver
calling card box,
1902. $24 £12

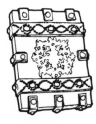

Victorian walnut and
ivory mounted card case,
10½cm. tall. $28 £14

Attractive mother-of-
pearl card case. $36 £18

Victorian mother-of-
pearl card case.$36 £18

Chinese ivory card
case with carved
panels. $40 £20

Tortoiseshell and
mother-of-pearl
card case. $44 £22

Chinoiserie decorated
tortoiseshell card case.
$44 £22

Silver card case,
Birmingham,
1907. $60 £30

A silver card case
by WN, Chester,
1903. $64 £32

Engine-turned
card case by Hilliard
and Thomason,
Birmingham, 1858.
$72 £36

Visiting card case
embossed with
golfer, Birmingham,
1906. $72 £36

Victorian silver
card case. $90 £45

Silver card and
notecase, with
propelling pencil,
by William Neale
& Sons, Sheffield,
1897. $128 £64

Birmingham silver
gilt card case, 1863,
4in. high. $160 £80

An electroplated
electrotype card
case by Elkington
Mason & Co, circa
1865, 4¼in. long.
$180 £90

A silver card case
embossed with a
design of Warwick
Castle, circa 1839.
$210 £105

25

CARDBOARD BOXES

Lever Brothers 'Lux soap flakes,
circa 1910. $6 £3

Lever Brothers 'Lifebuoy Soap',
circa 1910. $6 £3

Lever Brothers 'Sunlight Soap',
circa 1890. $6 £3

Songster needle box complete
with contents. $6 £3

Lever Brothers 'Plantol' soap,
circa 1900. $8 £4

Mackintosh's toffee shop,
circa 1930. $14 £7

A small Victorian wooden casket, with applied plaster seals. $44 £22

Yellow lacquer casket with two companion smaller boxes, probably Italian. $144 £72

A tortoiseshell and silver mounted casket, 15.5cm. wide. $190 £95

An Italian black metal casket with hinged cover, 13¼in. wide, 12½in. high. $230 £115

19th century Indonesian casket inlaid with bone, 20in. long. $264 £132

A rectangular Italian ebony casket, 14in. wide, 12in. high, circa 1775. $420 £210

27

CASKETS

Spanish rectangular inlaid tortoise-shell casket decorated with scrolls and flowers in silver pique and brass, 1749. $600 £300

A Komai type casket from the early 20th century. $1,010 £505

Rare Italian Renaissance casket, circa 1560, 1ft. 10½in. wide. $1,404 £780

Early 18th century, Norwegian silver casket by Harmen Antoni Reimers of Bergen, circa 1715, 2¼in. wide, 2oz.4dwt. $2,280 £1,140

A 17th century black and gold lacquered casket. $2,400 £1,200

17th century Italian rock crystal casket, 7in. long. $3,060 £1,700

17th century French red leather casket, 16in. long. $3,600 £2,000

Italian casket shaped foot warmer, 1730. $8,250 £4,125

28

19th century German fan-shaped trinket box, with hinged cover, 3.5cm. wide. $44 £22

19th century Dresden pen box with hinged cover, 17.5cm. long. $68 £34

Mid 19th century Capo-di-Monte box, the top painted with cherubs and flowers and the inside with flowers. $130 £65

Early Birmingham snuff box, mid 18th century, 2½in. diameter. $340 £170

'Cousin und Cousine' a fairing group mounted on a decorated box. $480 £240

French oval porcelain casket. $740 £370

A Sevres casket modelled as an open fan, 33cm. wide.$1,150 £575

Copenhagen porcelain snuff box with painted and gilt decoration. $2,160 £1,080

George III mahogany cheese dish with scroll ends, 42½cm. wide. $90 £45

Georgian mahogany cheese coaster. $120 £60

Partitioned cheese and bread coaster on original castors, 16in. long, circa 1765. $144 £72

Small George II mahogany cheese coaster on the original leather castors, 14in. long, circa 1750. $160 £8

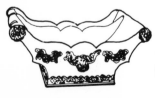

Mahogany cheese coaster with gilt decoration. $200 £100

George III mahogany cheese coaster. $200 £100

Tortoiseshell cigar case with elaborate gold pique decoration. $70 £35

Rosewood and ivory cigar box, circa 1840. $90 £45

An elephant's foot converted into a cigar and cigarette casket. $130 £65

An attractive Austrian cigar cabinet with sliding shelves and a locking front. $130 £65

Regency mahogany cigar box.
$340 £170

A silver Punch cigar lighter, London 1846, 12oz. $1,340 £670

31

CIGARETTE BOXES

Plated cigarette box with hinged cover, 17cm. wide. $20 £10

Oblong silver cigarette box with engraved inscription, 11.4cm. wide. $30 £15

An alabaster oblong cigarette box on gilt metal paw feet, 16cm. wide. $30 £15

Oblong silver cigarette box with hinged cover, 8½in. wide. $54 £27

Victorian silver smoker's companion. $90 £45

An onyx and brass mounted cigarette casket on ball feet, 7in. wide. $200 £100

Brass Tavern tobacco box with coin slot and engraved ship named 'Honour', circa 1830. $280 £140

Art Nouveau silver cigarette box by Omar Ramsden and Alwyn Carr, 5¾in. long. $820 £410

Cigar or cigarette case. $10 £5

Curved, silver cigarette case, Birmingham 1910, 4½oz. $20 £10

1930 s gentleman's cigarette case painted in grey, yellow and black. $24 £12

Art Deco metal cigarette case and compact with attached tassel, 10cm. long. $24 £12

Art Deco hand carved aluminium cigarette case. $24 £12

Victorian silver cigarette case. $24 £12

Concave shaped silver cigarette case with decoration on front and back, English, 1932. $68 £34

Oblong silver pocket cigarette case with enamelled portrait of a nude, 4oz.5dwt. $68 £34

CIGARETTE CASES

English metal cigarette case with flip-up top, 2¾in. x 3in. $68 £34

Tortoiseshell pale mottled cigarette case with a central cartouche of curling dragon and leaves. $120 £60

Unusual cigarette case of blue, orange and black lacquer on a silver base, 3in. x 5in. $360 £180

Unusual cigarette case and lighter combined, with enamel Chinese dragon design, late 1920's. $720 £36?

A Faberge cigarette case enamelled in white and green with gold mounts. $2,420 £1,210

Rectangular gold and enamel cigarette case, 3in. high, by Carl Faberge. $8,250 £4,125

Victorian country made oak
knife box. $24 £12

Georgian mahogany knife box,
with brass carrying handle. $68 £34

Early 19th century wooden
spoon rack. $72 £36

Mahogany and satinwood oblong
cutlery tray, 2ft. x 6½in. $104 £52

Georgian mahogany urn fully
fitted for cutlery. $320 £160

Pair of Sheraton period cutlery
urns. $800 £400

DECANTER BOXES

Small early 19th century mahogany decanter box containing four decanters. $110 £55

A George III satinwood and kingwood banded decanter box, the lid and front inlaid with shields, 7in.wide. $200 £100

Georgian mahogany decanter set with six Venetian gilt decorated spirit decanters, circa 1795.$230 £115

Coromandel and brass mounted liquor casket fitted with four cut glass decanters. $264 £132

Superb cased set of nine late 17th century cordial or spirit clear glass bottles in a wrought iron banded oak case, circa 1690. $1,080 £540

Early 18th century Austro-Hungarian octagonal casket containing twelve gilt decorated glass bottles, 26.5cm. wide.$1,100 £550

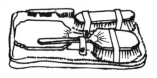

Four piece, lady's dressing table
set with enamelled mounts. $20 £10

Six piece silver mounted manicure
set in case. $24 £12

Victorian rosewood and brass
mounted vanity case. $48 £24

A coromandel and mother-of-
pearl inlaid dressing case with
glass and plated fittings. $100 £50

French mahogany travelling
vanity case, about 1850,
17½in. wide. $110 £55

Lady's cosmetic box in rosewood
with brass edging and stringing,
containing seven pieces of glass
and eight plated tops. $120 £60

DRESSING TABLE BOXES

Ornate silver set of dressing table equipment. $130 £65

Regency period brass bound rosewood toilet box with various bottles with plated tops. $150 £75

A late 19th century Indian ivory inlaid dressing box, the rim cross-banded in ivory and ebony, and the inlaid ivory interior is fitted with a mirror, 17in. wide. $170 £85

Coromandel box, Sheffield plate, with secret drawer. $220 £110

Turtle shell toilet set with Chinese dragon design, circa 1900-1910. $240 £120

Fitted dressing case with thirteen cut glass jars and bottles with Victorian silver tops. $360 £180

Lady's rosewood, brass-bound travelling toilet box, the glass jars and bottles with silver gilt lids, London, circa 1859. $380 £190

Late Art Nouveau painted eggshell enamel dressing set signed by N.H.
$600 £300

One of a pair of Irish silver toilet boxes and covers, Dublin 1700, by Thomas Boulton, 3¾in. diam., 12½oz. $1,250 £625

Travelling vanity case, about 1890, with lower drawer containing ivory backed brushes, 15in. long. $1,020 £510

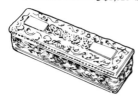

George III silver gilt rectangular toilet box by William Pitts, London 1815, 7in. long. $1,300 £650

Late Victorian vanity case in rosewood containing seventeen silver gilt pieces, 24in. long. $8,800 £4,400

White porcelain egg-shaped box decorated with painted flowers.
$40 £20

A miniature Bilston enamel egg, circa 1770. $180 £90

Silver nutmeg grater by KS. $264 £132

Oviform enamel box, the lid painted with a landscape, 1¾in. high.
$264 £132

A finely executed enamel bonbonniere.
$300 £150

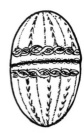

Late 18th century egg-shaped nutmeg grater by Samuel Meriton. $360 £180

An egg-shaped Bilston box decorated with flowers. $340 £170

Vienna enamel egg, hand painted with country scenes in the style of Wouvermans, 1.7/8in. diam. $420 £210

Pink enamel Faberge easter egg by Henrik Wigstrom. $165,000 £82,500

Bilston enamel box
with light blue base
and white lid. $40 £20

Bilston enamel box
with white lid and
blue base. $60 £30

Bilston box decorated
with a picture of a
lady. $160 £80

A rectangular,
Birmingham enamel
snuff box painted
with Juno and floral
decoration, 2in. wide.
$170 £85

Small hand-painted
box, inscribed with
a motto, made in
Bilston. $184 £92

Bilston enamel case
for a scent bottle.
$200 £100

Shoe shaped Bilston
box, 3½in. long.$220 £110

Magnificent deep
blue enamel rectan-
gular Battersea box.
$460 £230

French enamel box
designed as a 'Billet
Doux'. $460 £230

Unusual enamelled silver
box in the form of an
outsize matchbox, London
1905. $840 £420

Staffordshire, voyeurs
snuff box, 3¼in. wide,
circa 1765.
$920 £460

French gold and
enamel box, 1¾in.
$3,520 £1,760

41

ETUI

Ebony oval etui case with recesses for scissors, etc., in French hall-marked gold and silver. $160 £80

An unusual late 19th century book-shaped etui of tortoiseshell, ivory and silver, with a sliding end covering two inner containers. $180 £90

Etui and scent bottle modelled as a putto.
   $150 £75

An etui depicting a girl holding a basket, circa 1756.
   $220 £110

Mid 18th century jasper and gold mounted etui. $240 £120

Chelsea etui with harlequin head top, 12.5 in., circa 1760.
   $340 £170

Chelsea etui of cylindrical form, circa 1756.
   $360 £180

Late 18th century Staffordshire etui complete with thimble, needles and scissors. $800 £400

A rare 'Girl in a Swing' etui with Columbine head top, circa 1754.
   $1,400 £700

Louis XV gold etui by Jean Ducrollay of Paris, 1745-50.
   $6,600 £3,300

42

Dole cupboard with grill, for
storing bread, 20in. wide. $170 £85

French walnut food hutch,
circa 1780. $780 £390

French 18th century walnut bread
hutch, 32in. wide. $1,080 £540

Early oak food hutch. $1,560 £780

FREEDOM BOXES

A silver gilt Freedom box. $1,820 £910

Silver gilt Freedom casket by
Southampton to General Buller.
                $2,200 £1,100

George III Irish Freedom box, 3in.
wide, unmarked, circa 1795.
                $2,400 £1,200

George III Irish Freedom box, 3¼in.
wide, by Alexander Ticknell, Dublin
1797. $2,900 £1,450

GAMES BOXES

19th century Oriental carved wood games box. $100 £50

Victorian walnut games box.
$180 £90

Mid Victorian compendium of games. $530 £265

Indian ivory and ebony chess and backgammon board. $1,490 £745

English box and counters, 1755-1760, enamelled on copper, 6½cm. wide. $3,740 £1,870

Rare Louis XV gaming machine with the Louis Philippe Chateau mark, 5in. high. $19,800 £9,900

Small ruby glass box with metal
mounts and Mary Gregory
painting on lid. $68 £34

Bristol blue glass and silver
plate lidded drum, circa
1860. $140 £70

Palais Royal cut glass casket. $180 £90

Palais Royal cut glass casket on
hoof feet. $264 £132

Amber glass casket with ormolu
mounts and engraved with scenes,
10cm x 15cm, circa 1850. $300 £150

An English blue glass enamelled
snuff box made in the 1760's,
2¼in. wide. $1,560 £780

GOLD

French gold vinaigrette with enamelled floral decorations, by E.T. circa 1820. $420 £210

French gold snuff box with a chased floral border and central panel depicting two female figures. $770 £385

An antique Continental rock crystal shaped snuff box with gold mounts, 2¾in. wide. $890 £445

19th century Continental three-coloured gold snuff box. $1,320 £660

George III gold vinaigrette set with a gold citrine. $1,440 £720

Swiss gold snuff box, 3¼in. long. $1,440 £720

18ct. gold snuff box, 1803, 3in. long. $1,800 £900

Gold vinaigrette by W. and P. Cunningham, Edinburgh, 1814. $1,900 £950

Swiss gold, enamel and diamond snuff box, 3¼in. $2,400 £1,200

18th century gold and enamel snuff box with lid painted by Richter. $2,800 £1,400

A mid 18th century English snuff box of pudding stone mounted in gold. $4,400 £2,200

Late 18th century German gold snuff box, inset with hardstones, by Christian Neuber, 7.3cm. diam. $4,400 £2,200

Swiss gold and enamel automaton snuff box with watch $14,300 £7,150

Louis XVI octagonal gold snuff box, Paris 1774, 8.3cm. wide. $14,800 £7,400

Enamelled gold and paint on ivory snuff box by James Morriset, 1779, 8.9cm. wide. $18,480 £9,240

Louis XV mother-of-pearl encrusted snuff box made in Paris in 1759. $34,000 £17,000

Gold and enamelled box with pink and en grisaille panels about 1787, 2½in. wide. $40,000 £20,000

An 18th century French gold and enamel snuff box. $120,000 £60,000

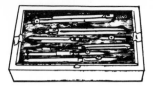

A set of architect's drawing instruments by Thornton Ltd., in mahogany case. **$50 £25**

A brass microscope with eyepiece and six objectives, in a mahogany case. **$96 £48**

A very fine 19th century sextant, by Lilley & Son, London, with platinum scale, and rosewood sighting handle, in original mahogany box. **$400 £200**

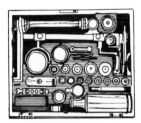

Early 19th century brass microscope by A. Abrahams of Liverpool. **$910 £455**

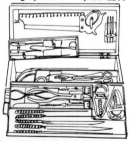

One of two brass bound mahogany cases of medical instruments, late 19th century, 43cm. wide. **$910 £455**

Early 19th century thirty hour chronometer by Dent of London. **$1,030 £515**

Japanese four case inro decorated in red, gold and black lacquer, signed Bunryusai. $180 £90

Three compartment inro decorated with a pair of silver cranes, signed Koma Kiuhaku.

$360 £180

An unsigned 19th century five case inro, decorated in gold hira-maki-e and other techniques, showing chrysanthemums beside a waterfall. $430 £215

Three case inro decorated in gold, red, grey and other coloured lacquers, signed Katikawa. $480 £240

Four case inro decorated with pine trees in various shades of gold with Mount Fuji in the background.

$540 £270

An inro of the mid Edo period, in the style of Korin, decorated with a trailing plant inlaid with mother-of-pearl and oxidised pewter. $720 £360

INROS

Five-case inro decorated with chrysanthemums and leaves in gold lacquer. $780 £390

A black lacquer inro signed Inagawa, decorated in gold and silver with waves, rocks and shells. $900 £450

A five-case inro signed Kajikawa, showing musical instruments and dance accoutrements. $1,150 £575

A four-case inro signed Shokosai, depicting crested and breaking waves. $1,200 £600

A gold lacquered five-case inro, decorated with metal, pearl and horn, depicting an immortal washing at a waterfall. $1,320 £660

Decorated inro or multiple belt box. $1,640 £820

A six-case inro, signed Koma Kyukaku, depicting a cockfight, with attached coral ojime and a netsuke, signed Zashin. $1,680 £840

A 19th century inro, signed Jokasi, decorated in gold, black, red and silver hira-maki-e with gongs on stands, with attached wood maju netsuke. $1,800 £900

A four-case inro, signed Kosai, decorated in gold, red and black lacquer, the details inlaid in ivory. $1,920 £960

An unsigned four-case inro decorated in gold and silver tatamaki-e, showing cranes flying and feeding, with attached metal and lacquer netsuke. $2,040 £1,020

A four-case, 19th century inro, signed Kakosai of Shozan, in various techniques of gold and black lacquer, inlaid in gold and mother-of-pearl. $2,400 £1,200

Vase shaped Japanese inro. $3,080 £1,540

51

INROS

A rare three-case inro signed
Jokasai and Yosei. $3,850 £1,925

An unusually shaped Japanese
inro. $5,500 £2,750

Five-case, burnished lacquer
inro by Kasen. $6,000 £3,000

Tachibana Gyokuzan and Suzuki
Tokoku inro. $17,000 £8,500

Early 19th century Japanese
lacquer inro by Shibata Zeshin,
4¾in. long. $14,000 £7,000

One of an excellent set of twelve
inros showing the Japanese signs
of the Zodiac. $34,000 £17,000

A pair of ivory glove stretchers in a rosewood inlaid oblong box. $30 £15

Indian box with ivory and silver inlay, about 1915. $30 £15

A late 19th century carved ivory flower box, with a basket-weave base and fitted with a gold hinge. $200 £100

A Persian chest shaped box with lion's paw feet, inlaid with ivory over a tortoiseshell ground, circa 1900. $100 £50

18th century cylindrical ivory gaming counter box with screw top cover. $240 £120

A fine Japanese ivory canister carved from one tusk, 3½in. high, circa 1850. $300 £150

53

An elephant tooth box by Hilliard
Thomasson, Birmingham, 1870,
9½ x 6½cm. $420 £210

An ivory and penwork tea casket,
Vizagapatam, circa1800. $620 £310

Indian ivory veneered small
cabinet, 18th century, 66cm.
wide. $1,320 £660

19th century French carved
ivory domed casket, with
copper gilt handles and lock.
          $2,420 £1,210

A carved ivory container
believed to be of 12th century
Coptic design. $4,400 £2,200

Interesting ivory casket, partly
15th century, partly 19th century,
10in. long. $11,700 £6,500

An unusual octagonal jewel box of coromandel with satinwood, ebony and kingwood banding, circa 1810. $96 £48

Regency Tunbridge ware jewellery casket in rosewood and boxwood, 9½in. long. $110 £55

Regency rosewood jewel box inlaid with brass. $130 £65

Mid 19th century French Second Empire ormolu jewel casket, signed C. De Franor, 10in. wide. $360 £180

17th century silver mounted tortoiseshell jewellery casket. $840 £420

Victorian black Moroccan covered jewel case with silver trim, by E.H.S., 1870. $2,700 £1,350

A mahogany knife box with shaped front, fitted as a stationery case, 14½in. high.
$90 £45

Late 18th century mahogany knife box. $170 £85

Late 18th century mahogany knife box with ornate brass keyhole escutcheon. $250 £125

George III mahogany knife box fitted with silver handled cutlery.
$380 £190

Late 18th century urn-shaped mahogany knife box. $500 £250

An exceptionally fine chinoiserie knife case. $2,400 £1,200

Victorian lacquered box decorated with mother-of-pearl. $20 £10

Japanese lacquered box decorated with flowers. $36 £18

Chinese black lacquered box, 15in. wide. $44 £22

Japanese lacquered box, 13½in. wide. $52 £26

Sarcophagus-shaped black and gold lacquer box with a scene of Chinese figures in a landscape. $48 £24

A late 18th century chinoiserie lacquer box, circa 1790. $100 £50

LACQUERED BOXES

A Kashmir lacquered box. $120 £60

Early 19th century lacquer games box with six lidded boxes and nine trays. $170 £85

Small square Oriental box in the Komai style, late 19th century.
$200 £100

19th century Japanese lacquer box. $220 £110

Late Georgian lacquer box with silver carrying handle. $230 £115

A cinnabar lacquer box and cover of the Ch'ien Lung period, carved in relief with blossoming branches on a key fret ground.
$340 £170

Japanese, 19th century lacquered
wood box and cover inscribed,
Shiomi Masanari, 17.3cm. long.
$1,500 £750

19th century English lacquer box
by Jennens and Bettridge. $410 £205

Japanese, late Edo period robe-chest
(hasami-bako) lacquer with metal
mounts, 58.5cm. wide. $5,000 £2,500

19th century Japanese rectangular
lacquer cabinet, 4in. high.
$5,500 £2,750

Fine Japanese lacquer workbox
and tray. $7,400 £3,700

A Louis XV lacquer snuff box,
3in. long. $34,000 £17,000

MATCH CASES

Match case commemorating the Silver Jubilee of George V and Queen Mary. $16 £8

Angel match box holder, Birmingham, 1903. $20 £10

Silver match case with fluted decoration. $36 £18

Silver match case with floral decoration. $50 £25

Metal match case in the form of a Gladstone bag. $70 £35

Vesta match case showing Edward VII, 1901. $100 £50

Victorian silver Vesta box with
embossed horse race scene.
$100 £50

A Daum match-holder of rectangular
form, the pale blue frosted glass
body enamelled with an Alpine
scene, 4cm. high. $100 £50

French Art Nouveau silver
smoker's set, circa 1900. $180 £90

Vesta match case advertising
Otto Monsteds Margarines.
$190 £95

Silver vesta case, 1913. $200 £100

Golfer match box by Sampson
Morden & Co., 1891. $420 £210

61

MISCELLANEOUS

Spectacle box made from papier mache inlaid with pewter, English, about 1860. $20 £10

Victorian inlaid mahogany shoe box. $24 £12

A mahogany oblong box with brass handle on lid, 12in. long. $32 £16

A walnut oblong box and cover, on fluted ball feet, 12in. wide. $32 £16

19th century Tunbridge ware handkerchief box depicting a stag. $52 £26

Mid 18th century ivory carved bodkin case. $60 £30

Wooden shoe with brass and copper pique, circa 1870. $70 £35

18th century elm taper box. $70 £35

Small, 19th century pony skin trunk. $84 £42

Mahogany hospital collection box with gilt lettering, circa 1840, 10in. high. $84 £42

An extremely fine Sheraton mahogany paint box with ebony stringing, containing the original paints and palettes, by Windsor and Newton, London. $100 £50

Tunbridge ware box which bears the trade label of Edmund Nye, early 19th century. $110 £55

Silver toilet box by Nathaniel Mills of Birmingham, 1849. $120 £60

Two Continental wicker oval military despatch cases, different, 18th century. $170 £85

George IV silver toothpick case, 2½in. wide, by Ledsam, Vale and Wheeler, Birmingham, 1827. $180 £90

Oblong ivory toothpick case, late 18th century, 3½in. wide $200 £100

A French walnut and kingwood oval shaped jardiniere with brass handles and borders, and inset china plaque and liner, 13in. wide. $210 £105

Silver box to hold a wax taper, about 1880, 1oz.75dwt. $300 £150

Fine silver comb box with pierced cover by William Parkin, London 1821, 6¾in. long. $480 £240

Kingwood ormolu mounted jardiniere, circa 1840, 46cm. wide. $830 £415

Chippendale octagonal mahogany bonnet box, circa 1760, 58cm. wide. $900 £450

Russian silver gilt and enamel throne salt container, about 1880. $3,960 £1,980

19th century Japanese wooden money box, with a landscaped panel in marquetry, 14cm. high. $30 £15

An automated 'Jolly Nigger' money bank. $40 £20

English china money box in the form of a pear. $44 £22

Miniature treasure chest in silver, Art Nouveau design, Birmingham, 1904. $110 £55

Late 19th century American cast iron 'Punch and Judy' money box, 7½in. high. $310 £155

17th century wrought iron money box. $1,440 £720

Scottish horn snuff mull with
a silver and onyx cover. $100 £50

Scottish mull, circa 1820,
10cm. long. $130 £65

Scottish snuff mull, circa 1800
$200 £100

Scottish snuff mull, circa 1790.
$240 £120

Scottish snuff mull, circa 1760.
$320 £160

Silver mounted ram's head table
snuff mull, about 1880, 13½in.
high. $820 £410

Victorian silver thimble in a mother-of-pearl case. $20 £10

Five manicure tools, in blue leather bag, 4in. long. $84 £42

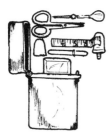

Ladies sewing case in brilliant blue papier mache, circa 1840, 3¾in. high. $160 £80

Early Victorian, European leather necessaire with an ivory plaque depicting a romanticised rural domestic scene. $170 £85

An 11½in. musical necessaire, in the form of a grand piano. $380 £190

French Empire ormolu and mother-of-pearl necessaire casket, with musical box.   £460

67

PATCH BOXES

Silver Georgian patch box, almond shaped and engraved with leaves and a shield enclosing the initials 'EB'. $80 £40

Ivory and gold pique patch box, mid 18th century. $100 £50

Miniature silver patch box by Samuel Pemberton, Birmingham, 1818. $110 £55

Late 18th century shoe bonbonniere, 2½in. high. $140 £70

A plated patch box with an enamel cover, circa 1760. $144 £72

Ivory patch box decorated with blue enamel, gold and pearls. $200 £100

Early 18th century circular patch box, ¾in. diam., by Thomas Kedder, London, circa 1705. $200 £100

Bilston enamel patch box on pink ground, about 1775. $200 £100

Queen Anne silver patch box, with
the image of Queen Anne and the
initials QA on cover, London, circa
1707, by T.Kedder. $200 £100

Oval enamel patch box, the lid
painted with a shepherd and
shepherdess, 1¾in. wide. $220 £110

Oval enamel patch box, the lid
painted with shipping by a quay,
2in. wide. $240 £120

Circular box, revolving to show
love scenes, 3½in. diam., circa
1820. $234 £130

Circular enamel patch box
modelled as a cat on a lilac
cushion, 1½in. diam. $350 £175

Birmingham patch box, 1¾in. wide,
circa 1760-65. $400 £200

Circular enamel patch box
modelled as a spaniel dog on
a powder blue cushion, 1½in.
diameter. $500 £250

Oval enamel patch box,
modelled as a lion, 2in.
wide. $620 £310

PEN BOXES

17th century cloisonne pen rest.
$600 £300

A fine silver mace shaped penner,
circa 1690, with slots for three
quills, maker W.B. $600 £300

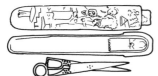

Persian lacquered
pen box. $700 £350

Pocket inkpot and penholder by
John Madin, Sheffield, 1656,
4in. long. $1,200 £600

Mid 19th century Persian pen
box decorated with figures.
$1,800 £900

Late 18th century papier mache
Qalamdan, Persian, 9½in. long.
$2,000 £1,000

Mid 19th century Persian pen
box decorated with seven large
panels of figure subjects.
$4,400 £2,200

Lacquer pen case
in the style of
Ali Quli Jabbadar.
$14,400 £7,200

Silver gilt Art Deco box with
enamel target design. $70 £35

High quality silver box with swirl
design, Birmingham 1892. $80 £40

Oval silver box having porcelain
lid with picture of a lady. $84 £42

Circular silver pill box, imported
by H.C.F., London 1903. $100 £50

Round silver pill box with kitten
enamelled on the lid. $110 £55

Victorian silver skull pill box.
$230 £115

71

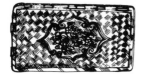

Victorian brass pin case. $12 £6

19th century wooden needle case
and thread spool. $12 £6

19th century Tunbridge ware pin
box. $34 £17

19th century tortoiseshell pin case
with a 'Renaissance' miniature on
either side. $100 £50

Pair of 19th century German
china pin boxes entitled
Grandmama and Grandpapa.
               $160 £80

Tortoiseshell and silver pique
box, Queen Anne. $190 £95

A coaching tavern post box of japanned tole ware, divided into three compartments, 13in. long, 5in. deep, 6½in. high. $44 £22

A miniature oak court cupboard, used as a posting box. $54 £27

19th century posting box engraved 'Cleared at 12am and 4pm'. $144 £72

Victorian red tin country house posting box, with gold lettering 'The Fawcett' and rate of postage.
$170 £85

A country house Royal Mail letter-box in pinewood, simulated to appear as mahogany, original black and gilt word 'Letters', 24½in. high. $240 £120

Oak country house letter box formed as a miniature pillar box, 16in. high. $310 £155

A small round gold filigree
inlaid tortoiseshell case. $60 £30

Art Deco silver box, a powder
compact, textured lid slashed
with red and black enamel. $76 £38

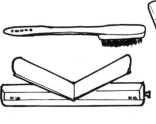

George II silver toothbrush and
double-sided powder box,
Birmingham 1801. $220 £110

Set of cigarette case, match box
and compact in green and black
enamel. $230 £115

Jamaican tortoiseshell powder
box with crest, 1636. $480 £240

Gold and enamel powder box,
Paris 1781, depicting a tree,
3in. diam. $4,400 £2,200

Victorian silver purse. $40 £20

Victorian bead purse. $20 £10

Late 19th century handbag with mother-of-pearl flowers and gilt clasp. $44 £22

A tortoiseshell and ivory mounted combined purse and peacock feather fan. $44 £22

A delicate 19th century tortoiseshell purse with decoration in gold pique point. $72 £36

La Minauderie; silver engine-turned evening bag by C. van Cleef and Arpels, about 1935.
$960 £480

Victorian burr walnut and
parquetry sewing box. $50 £25

Tunbridge ware sewing box. $60 £30

A Chinese black and gold lacquered
octagonal box, the interior fitted
with a tray with open and lidded
compartments, 14in. wide. $96 £48

Regency mahogany sewing box
with fitted interior. $110 £55

A Regency black lacquer sewing
casket, interior with compartments
and a drawer in the base, 14in.
wide. $120 £60

19th century 'antler' sewing box
with ivory compartments, 14in.
wide. $324 £180

Victorian oak smoker's box. $30 £15

Victorian oak smoker's cabinet
with Doulton tobacco jar. $54 £27

Victorian inlaid oak smoker's
cabinet, 39cm. high. $60 £30

Art Nouveau smoker's
cabinet with brass
facings, circa 1920,
1ft. 9in. high. $76 £38

'Ye Dragon of Wantley' - silver
mounted horn, smoker's companion
by Walker and Hall, Sheffield, 1916.
$180 £90

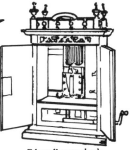

Edwardian smoker's
cabinet Alexandra
disc musical box. $1,240 £620

SNUFF BOXES

Papier mache snuff box with mother-of-pearl decoration. $20 £10

Victorian papier mache snuff box. $24 £12

Cowrie shell snuff box with silver mounts. $40 £20

Papier mache snuff box with a rim, decorated with a nicely painted domestic scene.$48 £24

Mussel shell snuff box mounted with silver. $68 £34

Shell snuff box, by Jonathan Millidge, Edinburgh, circa 1830, 7cm. long. $130 £65

Silver snuff box by Ed. Edwards, London, 1845.$130 £65

Silver oval snuff box by Samuel Pemberton, Birmingham 1799. $160 £80

An early 19th century snuff box in the shell of a tortoise. $170 £85

78

An unmarked mother-of-pearl topped and bottomed silver snuff box, English, circa 1760. $180 £90

Snuff box, by Wm. Purse, London, 1810. $180 £90

George IV silver snuff box, Birmingham 1827, by J. Betteridge, 3½in x 1¾in.
            $200 £100

Curved snuff box by Joseph Taylor, Birmingham 1806, in silver. $220 £110

Continental enamel snuff box in the form of a tricorn hat. $230 £115

Standing snuff box by J. Hewitt, Edinburgh, circa 1790, 18cm. high. $230 £115

Georgian oval table snuff box with onyx set hinged cover, and horned support, Dundee, circa 1830. $280 £140

George IV silver gilt snuff box.
    $300 £150

A fine silver shoe snuff box by EHS, London, 1876, 8½cm. long, 4½cm. high.
    $324 £162

SNUFF BOXES

Cowrie shell snuff box with one side of mother-of-pearl, about 1750. $320 £160

Silver pocket snuff box by Ambrose Stevenson, about 1720. $320 £160

Early 19th century silver snuff box by Charles Rawlings, 1820, 3in. long. $340 £170

Snuff box by S.P., Birmingham, 1781. $370 £185

A rare unmarked double snuff box, London 1730, 7½ x 5½cm. $420 £210

Victorian oval shaped snuff box by Nathaniel Mills, Birmingham, 1843. $500 £250

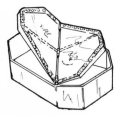

Octagonal silver snuff box by Phipps and Robinson, London 1791, 3oz. 25dwt. $540 £270

Silver snuff box by F.A., London, 1739, 6cm. long. $560 £280

A silver gilt snuff box by Nathaniel Mills, Birmingham 1834. $600 £300

Silver snuff box by Nathaniel Mills, depicting 'Abbotsford House', Birmingham 1838. $820 £410

George IV oval snuff box by Edward Cornelius Farrell, London 1822, 2¾in. wide. $910 £455

Fine silver snuff box by T.S., Birmingham 1830. $1,020 £510

Table snuff box with engine turned sides, T.H., J.H., Chester 1819, 4in. wide. $1,320 £660

Early 17th century Jacobite snuff box, 2¼in. diam., circa 1715. $1,380 £690

Silver snuff box in the shape of a fox's head, 3¼in. long, by Joseph Willmore, Birmingham 1834. $1,800 £900

Victorian silver snuff box. $1,560 £780

Silver snuff box in the form of a tortoise, by Wallis and Hayne, London 1820, 1822, 3¼in. long. $2,200 £1,100

Early 19th century Swiss musical box, snuff box and watch, 7cm. wide. $9 000 £4,500

SOUVENIR BOXES

Late 19th century transfer printed string holder . $20 £10

A late 19th century transfer-printed souvenir box. $20 £10

Wooden scent case with a glass bottle, made by Breadalbane Woods. $20 £10

Satinwood box with a water-colour picture of a spa painted on top, circa 1830. $60 £30

SOVEREIGN CASES

Victorian metal sovereign case.
                      $20 £10

Bean-shaped sovereign case in silver, Birmingham 1904. $160 £80

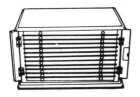

Mahogany coin cabinet of twelve
drawers, 12in. $80 £40

A pine watchmaker's cabinet,
circa 1800, 23in. high, 12in.
wide, 7½in. deep. $130 £65

A large collection of birds eggs in
pinewood cabinet of eight drawers,
1ft.7in. wide, 3ft.1in. high. $144 £72

A superb 19th century burr walnut
specimen box with eighteen drawers.
                            $430 £215

George III hardwood collector's
cabinet, the single glazed door
enclosing fourteen small drawers,
1ft.10in. wide. $720 £360

An extremely rare George III
numismatist's table cabinet, cross-
banded with satinwood, furnished
with sixty trays in two banks,
circa 1770-80. $1,200 £600

SPICE BOXES

Table square spice box with named sectioned interior, circa 1840. $80 £40

Circular table spice box complete with nutmeg grater, circa 1830, 7in. diam. $84 £42

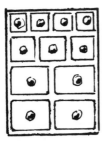

Pinewood spice drawers with brass pulls, circa 1820, 14½in. high x 11½in. x 7in. $132 £66

George I walnut spice cabinet, 21in. high. $200 £100

An oak spice cupboard with eight interior drawers, circa 1670. $320 £160

Small yew wood spice box, crossbanded and with double herringbone inlay, circa 1700. $720 £360

Victorian brass stamp box. $6 £3

Sterling silver stamp envelope, Chester 1907. $24 £12

A sledge shaped silver stamp box, Birmingham, 1908. $48 £24

Ivory and tortoiseshell box, early 19th century. $120 £60

STRING HOLDERS

Yew wood string holder. $24 £12

Yew wood string holder with ridged decoration. $28 £14

STATIONERY BOXES

Victorian inlaid mahogany
stationery box. $30 £15

A Victorian velvet and brass
mounted stationery case,
9in. wide. $44 £22

A coromandel wood oblong
stationery box with domed cover
and brass mounts. $48 £24

Tooled leather writing paper
cabinet, with original brass key
escutcheon and lock, by W.
Houghton, Stationer, Bond Street,
6½in. long. $48 £24

Victorian leather and silver
mounted stationery case.
                $100 £50

19th century Tunbridge ware
stationery box. $110 £55

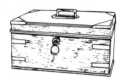

A Victorian mahogany brass bound strongbox, the interior with a removeable lockable money tray, 1ft.2in. wide. $72 £36

Brass cash box with handle on the cover, 11½in. $116 £58

An interesting American civil war period Naval Paymaster's strongbox, 12 x 8 x 6in. $220 £110

17th century German iron strongbox, the lid and sides overlaid with trellis work and painted with roses. $910 £455

Late 17th century Dutch iron strongbox, 27½in. high. $1,320 £660

17th century Spanish iron chest, 31in. wide, with floral painted panels. $1,680 £840

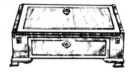

A miniature walnut inlaid bureau, with a drawer, on bracket feet, 17¾in. wide. $180 £90

17th century oak desk, I.N., 1636. $190 £95

An oak desk box with a hinged sloping front above stylised geometric carving, circa 1690. $220 £110

A George II mahogany table bureau with tambour top and brass carrying handles. $240 £120

A fine William and Mary table desk, in yew wood, 21in. long, 17in. high. $860 £430

Oak table desk with original handles circa 1700, 36cm. wide. $1,080 £540

A birch oblong tea caddy, decorated with transfer printed view of Ford Castle. $36 £18

Georgian mahogany tea caddy with a brass handle and boxwood inlay.
$36 £18

A Victorian rosewood oblong sarcophagus shaped tea caddy, 11in. wide. $44 £22

Mahogany oblong tea caddy with satinwood shell motifs, 7½in. $44 £22

Victorian birds' eye maple tea caddy, 12in. wide. $54 £27

Walnut oblong tea caddy with domed cover. $54 £27

A fruitwood sarcophagus
shaped tea caddy, circa
1820. $64 £32

.A Georgian mahogany oblong
ogee shaped tea caddy with brass
handle. $70 £35

Victorian mahogany and brass
bound tea caddy inset with
white stones. $72 £36

19th century tortoiseshell tea
caddy on bun feet. $72 £36

Tunbridge ware tea caddy. $72 £36

Banded mahogany and ebony
string inlay domed top tea
caddy with a glass liner. $84 £42

19th century tortoiseshell tea caddy with brass line inlay. $84 £42

Regency casket-shaped mahogany tea caddy, on brass ball feet, circa 1820. $84 £42

Regency brass inlaid tea caddy. $84 £42

Small early 19th century inlaid mahogany tea caddy. $84 £42

Sheraton mahogany tea caddy, with satinwood and ivory key escutcheon, on bun feet, circa 1805, 12in. long, 6in. wide, 6½in. high. $84 £42

A Regency rosewood and sarcophagus shaped tea caddy, the interior with two lidded compartments flanking the mixing bowl. $84 £42

A Chinese black, red and gold lacquer octagonal tea caddy, the interior fitted with two pewter containers, 14in. wide. $84 £42

Regency brass inlaid mahogany tea caddy. $84 £42

Sheraton period partridgewood tea caddy, circa 1800. $90 £45

A Chinese black lacquer octagonal tea caddy, decorated with figures, in gold, fitted with two pewter containers, 11in. wide. $90 £45

Serpentine fronted tortoiseshell tea caddy. $90 £45

Tortoiseshell two division tea caddy with ivory feet, 18.5cm. wide. $100 £50

19th century shaped tortoiseshell
tea caddy. $100 £50

Small tortoiseshell tea caddy,
12cm. wide. $100 £50

Rosewood two division tea
caddy strung with boxwood
decoration , 21cm wide. $100 £50

Early Victorian mahogany tea
caddy inlaid with mother-of-
pearl decoration. $100 £50

Victorian parquetry tea caddy
with glass liner. $100 £50

Georgian mahogany tea caddy
with herringbone inlay and
brass carrying handle. $100 £50

Serpentine mahogany tea caddy
with chevron crossbanding
and original handle, 8½ x 5in.,
circa 1780. $100 £50

Tortoiseshell two division tea
caddy strung with pewter and
applied with mother-of-pearl,
20cm. wide. $100 £50

19th century octagonal, black
and gilt lacquered two division
caddy in the Chinese style. $100 £50

Two of six black japanned tea
canisters, decorated with
Chinese gilt design, 17in. high.
$100 £50

Part of a set of six green
japanned tea canisters, 17in.
high. $100 £50

Small 19th century tortoiseshell
tea caddy with brass feet. $100 £50

Victorian rosewood sarcophagus shaped tea caddy with a glass bowl. $104 £52

Sheraton mahogany tea caddy, 19cm. wide. $110 £55

Early 19th century rosewood tea caddy inlaid with brass. $110 £55

Fine quality 19th century walnut and brass mounted tea caddy with a glass liner. $110 £55

A fine Chippendale period mahogany tea caddy, containing three compartments and secret drawer. $116 £58

Tortoiseshell two division tea caddy strung with pewter, 15.5cm. wide. $116 £58

TEA CADDIES

Sheraton fiddle back mahogany tea caddy, 11.5cm. wide. $120 £60

18th century mahogany caddy with painted oval medallions. $120 £60

Russian hand painted papier mache tea caddy with maker's name in the foiled interior. $120 £60

19th century Tunbridge ware domed tea caddy. $120 £60

Sheraton inlaid tea caddy. $120 £60

Late 18th century satinwood tea caddy crossbanded in kingwood. $130 £65

Mid Victorian rectangular painted and gilt papier mache tea caddy, 13in wide. $130 £65

Early Victorian tortoiseshell tea caddy. $130 £65

Sheraton yew wood two division tea caddy, 19cm. wide. $130 £65

A Sheraton satinwood and inlaid tea caddy, circa 1790. $144 £72

Tortoiseshell two division tea caddy inlaid with mother-of-pearl, 8in. wide. $144 £72

19th century tortoiseshell tea caddy. $144 £72

Tortoiseshell two division tea caddy inlaid with mother-of-pearl, 22cm. wide. $144 £72

Yew wood two division tea caddy inlaid with mother-of-pearl, 22cm. wide. $144 £72

Large 19th century Tunbridge ware caddy. $160 £80

Early 19th century papier mache tea caddy. $160 £80

Adam style satinwood and marquetry octagonal tea caddy decorated with urns swags and flowers, 5 x 4in., circa 1785. $170 £85

George III satinwood tea caddy with marquetry inlay, about 1780, 5in. high. $170 £85

Rosewood tea caddy inlaid
with mother-of-pearl. $170 £85

Late 18th century harewood tea
caddy inlaid with satinwood. $180 £90

18th century octagonal caddy of
curled paper design with leaf
sprays. $180 £90

Sheraton style tea caddy of
satinwood and rosewood,
circa 1795. $180 £90

Sheraton period satinwood tea
caddy with ebony string inlay.
                           $180 £90

Two division mother-of-pearl
caddy on ivory feet. $180 £90

TEA CADDIES

Tortoiseshell two division tea caddy, 17.5cm. wide. $180 £90

A large, fine quality, Tunbridge ware tea caddy. $184 £92

George III tea caddy veneered in rolled paper, 18cm. wide. $200 £100

Oval caddy in satinwood cross-banded with rosewood and inlaid with harewood, circa 1800. $200 £100

Sheraton mahogany caddy inlaid with roses. $220 £110

Sheraton fiddle back mahogany two division tea caddy inlaid with marquetry, 17.5cm. wide. $220 £110

Queen Anne tea caddy of veneered walnut on oak with chevron cross-banding on the lid and original handle and escutcheon, circa 1700, 9in. long. $240 £120

Large tea caddy in figured mahogany, 21in. high. $260 £130

Georgian fruitwood tea caddy in the shape of a pear, and with its original lock and key. $290 £145

George III fruitwood tea caddy in the form of an apple. $300 £150

Sheraton period satinwood inlaid octagonal tea caddy with paperwork and glazed panels, 17cm. wide. $310 £155

Ivory Tea caddy with rosewood stringing. $330 £165

George III oval harewood tea
caddy, 5½in. wide. $360 £180

George III inlaid satinwood
caddy with silver mounted
glass containers. $360 £180

18th century satinwood
rectangular casket with inlaid
panels designed with shells,
containing two rectangular
caddies. $392 £186

George III harewood and
marquetry caddy with flower
vignettes, about 1790, 5in.
high. $430 £215

Early mahogany caddy case with
original tin caddies inside, 4in.
high. $440 £220

Rare Pontypool oval tea caddy
painted in gilt and red, about
1780, 5½in. high. $470 £235

Fine Regency caddy of pen work illustrating 'The Fortune Teller', 5in. high. $470 £235

19th century Dutch marquetry octagonal tea chest, 13in. wide. $530 £265

Late 18th century decagonal tea caddy of tortoiseshell with ivory banding and a silvered plaque, 5in. high. $560 £280

Mahogany urn-shaped caddy, circa 1790, 9in. high, with ivory finial. $640 £320

Caddy box with two caddies and a glass bowl, about 1820, 6in. high. $660 £330

Rare early Georgian caddy case of wood covered with shagreen and mounted with silver, 7in. high. $660 £330

TEA CADDIES

Red Tole ware tea caddy with two canisters, English, about 1790, 5¾in. high. $720 £360

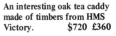

An interesting oak tea caddy made of timbers from HMS Victory. $720 £360

Very rare late 18th century rolled paper tea caddy, English about 1790, 5in. high. $890 £445

Rare 18th century ivory tea caddy in carved and pierced ivory with handle, about 1790, 5½in. high. $1,130 £565

Fine late 18th century tea caddy entirely veneered in mother-of-pearl with silver handles and ball and claw feet, 6½in. high. $1,200 £600

One of a pair of George III canteloup-shaped tea caddies, 4½in. wide. $1,440 £800

104

Art Deco Chinamen tea caddy.
$20 £10

19th century ruby glass circular
box and cover, 4in. $70 £35

Victorian slagware caddy, circa
1870, 5½in. high. $110 £55

An early 19th century Worcester
teapoy. $200 £100

K'ang Hsi enamelled tea caddy on
bracket feet but without cover.
$290 £145

A Lowestoft porcelain tea
caddy, with chinoiserie
decoration. $410 £205

Meissen tea caddy and cover, 10 5cm.. high, circa 1740, numeral 19 impressed. $560 £280

K'ang Hsi tea caddy of rectangular form, 4½in. high, on bracket feet. $720 £360

Rare Coalport 'jewelled' tea caddy on a pink ground, printed crown mark, 1890-1910, 6in. high. $840 £420

Fine Whieldon tea caddy of about 1745-50 with decorative panels, 5in. high. $1,140 £570

Meissen tea caddy and cover, 10.5cm. high, circa 1725. $1,700 £850

A pair of Staffordshire opaque white glass tea caddies, 14.2cm. high. $5,000 £2,500

George III plated tea caddy. $36 £18

Silver plated tea caddy. $90 £45

One of a pair of early 19th
century Sheffield plate tea
caddies. $110 £55

Sheffield plate caddy with a solid
silver plate engraved with a crest
set into the front, 1800-10, 4½in.
high. $110 £55

Sheffield plate caddy, about
1775-80, with typical Adam
decoration, and, unusually, a
lock. $200 £100

Oval Sheffield plate tea caddy,
4½in. wide, with bright cut
engraving. $340 £170

Late Victorian silver tea caddy,
11oz. $100 £50

A Continental silver, square,
tapering tea caddy and cover,
5½in. high, 7oz. $100 £50

Silver caddy by George Fox,
London 1898, 4in. high. $160 £80

Early 19th century silver tea
caddy, 12oz. $410 £205

An oval silver tea caddy by
Thomas Daniel, 1790, 14oz.
                    $480 £240

A silver Portuguese tea caddy
by P.I.E. Porto, circa 1810. $500 £250

George II silver tea caddy, of bombe form, embossed and chased with scrolls and foliage, 10oz., London 1752, 5¼in. high, made by S. Herbert & Co. $550 £275

George III oval shaped silver tea caddy with beaded edges and urn finial, by Aug. Le Sage, London 1779, 11½oz. $720 £360

A nicely shaped silver tea caddy by I.P.G., dated 1762. $740 £370

Silver tea canister by Joseph Fainell, 1720. $780 £390

A small bright cut silver tea caddy by R. Hennell, London 1791.
                          $1,010 £505

George III two-division tea caddy by Daniel Pontifex, London 1797, 19oz.13dwt., 7in. high. $1,010 £505

George III tea caddy, marked on base and cover, by Robert Hennell, London 1782, 4in. high, 13oz.2dwt. $1,060 £530

George III cylindrical tea caddy, 4¾in. high, marked on base and lid by Augistin le Sage, London 1767, 15oz.13dwt. $1,300 £650

George III shaped, oval tea caddy by T. Chauner, London 1785, 12oz.4dwt. $1,390 £695

An exceptionally fine set of George III silver caddies. $1,630 £815

A pair of George III silver bombe shaped tea caddies and rosewood casket. $1,680 £840

Pair of tea caddies and a mixing bowl by Samuel Taylor, London 1755, 27oz.15dwt., in a veneered rosewood case. $1,800 £900

Set of three George II tea caddies, maker Samuel Taylor, London 1746/7. $2,200 £1,100

18th century Dutch silver tea caddy, maker's mark I.B., Amsterdam, 1726, 8oz.7dwt. $2,280 £1,140

Set of three George II silver gilt tea caddies by Alexander Johnston, London 1754, 34oz.13dwt., in a silver mounted tortoiseshell case. $3,080 £1,540

Set of three George III tea caddies in case. $3,490 £1,745

Set of three silver tea caddies by John Chivers of Birmingham. $3,960 £1,980

Pair of George III silver caddies by Parket and Wakelin, London 1767, in a Japanese lacquered case. $5,940 £2,970

TIN BOXES

Miniature tin of Andrews Liver Salts produced by LNER trains, circa 1930. $8 £4

Caleys Jazz-time toffee tin, circa 1920. $12 £6

A large confectionery tin by John Buchanan, Glasgow, 8¾in. wide, circa 1890. $16 £8

Rowntree's toffee tin, circa 1930. $16 £8

Decorated mustard tin showing National Games. $34 £17

English tin container in the form of a commode chest, circa 1890-1910. $80 £40

Late 19th century English terracotta tobacco jar, 5in. tall. $36 £18

A circular carved wood tobacco jar. $40 £20

18th century lead tobacco jar of octagonal shape with scroll decorative bands around the top and bottom rims of the base, 5¼in. high, 5in. long. $68 £34

Liberty pewter and enamel tobacco box with sides cast with rows of stylised leaves and set with blue-green enamel cabochons, 4¾in. $100 £50

Dutch silver tobacco box with serpentine ends by Hendrina Das, Amsterdam, 1746, 5¼in. long. $2,420 £1,210

18th century Dutch oval tobacco box, 4½in. wide. $13,200 £6,600

113

TORTOISESHELL

Tortoiseshell box with plain shell sides and a mottled lid, inset with a pique daisy motif.
$48 £24

A small tortoiseshell case with gold filigree inlay. $144 £72

18th century gold and tortoiseshell pique work, circular snuff box, 2in. diam. $460 £230

Louis XV tortoiseshell and gold pique snuff box decorated all over with pique work of decreasing size, about 1725. $790 £39

17th century mother-of-pearl and tortoiseshell box, 19in. wide. $1,440 £720

An octagonal tortoiseshell snuff box, set with gold, jewels and enamel, 3in. wide. $3,300 £1,650

Early 20th century green and gold metal box, 4cm. high. $20 £10

A Victorian china trinket box. $30 £15

Silver trinket box with inlaid tortoiseshell lid. $48 £24

Victorian silver trinket box. $70 £35

Late 19th century silver trinket box, circa 1894. $120 £60

Basket shaped box with metal handles. $190 £95

VINAIGRETTES

William IV oblong engine-turned vinaigrette, Birmingham 1833, 2cm. wide. $80 £40

Silver gilt vinaigrette, by Joseph Willmore, Birmingham, 1807. $130 £65

Engine-turned vinaigrette with ring end, 1¼in. long, London 1821, maker WE. $220 £110

George III oval silver-gilt vinaigrette, 1¼in. wide, London 1800. $260 £130

George III snuff box cum vinaigrette, 2¼in. wide, by R. Lockwood and J. Douglas, London 1802. $400 £200

Silver vinaigrette by Nathaniel Mills. $460 £230

Silver vinaigrette by Nathaniel Mills depicting Warwick Castle in high relief, Birmingham 1837. $540 £270

Silver snuff box cum vinaigrette by William Shaw, Birmingham 1806. $720 £360

Victorian leather bound workbox with brass mounts and paw feet.
$36 £18

A Cairo carved wood and ivory workbox, with fitted interior, 13in. wide.
$36 £18

A Victorian rosewood inlaid and marquetry oblong workbox, 13in. wide.
$48 £24

Lady's satinwood workbox, with ebony stringing and oval key escutcheon, circa 1795. $84 £42

Japanese black lacquered octagonal workbox with hinged cover, 15½in. wide.
$90 £45

Lacquered workbox with lift-up lid and four drawers. $380 £190

117

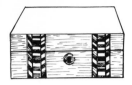

Late 19th century inlaid walnut
writing box. $40 £20

A mahogany and brass bound
portable writing desk, 18in. wide.
                          $44 £22

A Victorian mahogany and brass
bound portable writing desk, 16in.
                          $44 £22

Victorian walnut veneered writer's
companion with a brass carrying
handle and fitted drawer. $50 £25

An oblong portable writing desk,
14in. wide. $54 £27

Silver mounted writing set of
letter opener, pen and knife,
seal and two ink bottles. $54 £27

Victorian walnut writing cabinet with brass mounts. $60 £30

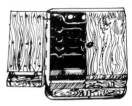

Victorian burr walnut writing slope with a fitted interior. $60 £30

A Victorian walnut writing box of well figured wood with brass mounted corners. $60 £30

Walnut and brass bound portable writing desk, 19½in. $68 £34

An unusual Victorian writing box, the exterior applied overall with bands of porcupine quills, 1ft.3in. wide. $72 £36

Victorian rosewood and mother-of-pearl inlaid portable writing desk, 15in. wide. $72 £36

119

WRITING BOXES

Victorian rosewood portable writing desk, with mother-of-pearl inlay and carved, beaded borders.
$84 £42

Regency period rosewood writing slope.
$84 £42

A Victorian walnut portable writing desk, with ebony and mother-of-pearl inlaid border, 16in. wide.
$84 £42

19th century Japanese lacquered portable writing desk decorated in gilt, 44cm. wide.
$88 £44

19th century inlaid walnut writing box.
$88 £44

Victorian inlaid rosewood writing case with fitted interior.
$90 £45

Victorian burr walnut writing cabinet with three drawers and gilt brass fittings. $96 £48

19th century Tunbridge ware writing slope. $120 £60

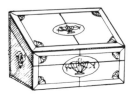

Georgian mahogany travelling desk inlaid with satinwood. $144 £72

An officer's document case, in brass banded mahogany, with flush inset carrying handles, original Bramah lock by Muckleston Patent. $144 £72

19th century desk set containing pen, paper knife and seal, 8½in. x 3½in. $160 £80

Regency period camphorwood writing slope with brass fittings. $160 £80

WRITING BOXES

Good quality Regency brass inlaid writing box. $170 £85

A·fine 19th century coromandel wood brass bound lap desk. $180 £90

18th century French papier mache writing box. $300 £150

An unusual Victorian papier mache and decorated writing cabinet containing a workbox, writing slide and small drawers. $360 £180

Inside lid of a suzuribako (writing box) lacquered in gold. $3,520 £1,760

Louis XV ormolu encrier with brass inlaid ebony frieze, 1ft. 11in. wide. $4,000 £2,000

Index